Original title:
The Birch's Ballad

Copyright © 2025 Creative Arts Management OÜ
All rights reserved.

Author: Colin Leclair
ISBN HARDBACK: 978-1-80566-726-1
ISBN PAPERBACK: 978-1-80566-855-8

Dance of the White Tree

In the forest where all trees play,
A white tree dances in a funny way.
It sways and twirls like a ballet star,
Pulling leaves with laughter from near and far.

Squirrels giggle and share a glance,
As the tree invites them to join the dance.
With a rustle and shake, they jump right in,
Laughing together, let the fun begin!

Swaying in the Gentle Breeze

Underneath the skies so blue,
Trees sway like they're in a zoo.
Branches wave like arms on high,
Telling jokes to the passing sky.

Leaves whistle tunes of sheer delight,
In the breeze, they find their flight.
Robins chirp in perfect key,
Swaying along with such glee!

The Song of Resilient Roots

Roots tickle the ground, they hum a tune,
Staying strong under the silly moon.
They whisper stories of days gone past,
With every chuckle, their joy will last.

Through thick and thin, they dance in place,
A merry jig full of grace.
No storm can shake their funny groove,
With roots so bold, they always move!

Tranquil Murmurs of the Tall Ones

Tall trees chuckle, whispering low,
Sharing secrets that only they know.
Breezes carry their laughter wide,
As woodland critters join the ride.

With a rustling chorus, they sing a song,
Those tall ones remind us: we all belong.
In their embrace, we find our cheer,
In dancing shadows, joy is near!

Chronicle of Rustling Fronds

In a forest where whispers tread,
Leaves tell tales of laughter and dread.
A squirrel danced on a twig so spry,
The frogs croaked tunes on the fly.

A frog donned a hat made of bark,
He sang to the moon until it was dark.
Birds chimed in a harmonious shout,
'Tis the funniest show, without a doubt!'

Solace Among the Sturdy Pines

Amidst the pines, tall and proud,
A raccoon juggled nuts to the crowd.
A deer with a grin, quite absurd,
Said, 'Join in the fun, don't miss a word!'

The owls hooted with glee above,
As critters waltzed, showing their love.
The night was alive, a charming scene,
With giggling leaves in vibrant green.

Charms of the Silver-Limbed

Silver limbs swayed with a playful grace,
Each twist and turn held a game or a race.
A chipmunk scampered in a comical reel,
Stashing acorns, an acorn-filled meal.

The breeze whispered secrets of day's delight,
As shadows danced in the moon's gentle light.
Laughter rang out, a lovely refrain,
Echoing joy amidst nature's domain.

Life Beneath the Starlit Canopy

Beneath the stars, where fireflies blink,
Creatures gather to chat and to drink.
A wise old owl with spectacles found,
Exclaimed, 'When did nighttime become so profound?'

Mice in tuxedos danced 'round the rock,
While crickets strummed a melodious clock.
Every moment sprouted a chuckle or cheer,
In this whimsical world, joy thrives here.

The Wisdom of Whispering Leaves

Leaves giggle in the breeze,
Sharing secrets with the trees.
Branches dance in goofy glee,
Nature's laughter, wild and free.

Roots tickle the ground below,
Saying jokes only they know.
Sunlight shines with a cheeky wink,
As shadows play and dance and blink.

Fragments of Wood's Ancient Song

Woodpeckers drum a silly beat,
On hollow trunks, they take a seat.
Squirrels chatter their playful tune,
While frogs croak under the moon.

Branches sway in jovial jest,
While mossy cushions offer rest.
The forest hums a tune so bright,
Making woodland creatures bite!

In Praise of the Wind-Swept Canopy

Up above, the leaves play tag,
Telling tales that never lag.
Wind swoops in with a joyful shout,
Making sure no fun's left out.

Clouds join in with a fluffy cheer,
Whirling 'round, they bring us near.
Together they form a jolly crew,
Creating laughter, bright and new.

The Forgotten Stories of Vibrant Bark

Bark holds tales of days gone past,
Of brave explorers and spells cast.
In every crevice, a giggle hides,
Pirate treasures hid inside!

Twisted knots form a silly face,
Ancient mischief fills this place.
When storms rage and branches creak,
The trees just laugh, and never speak.

Mosaics of Green and Gold

In a dance of shades and hue,
Leaves wave like they know what to do.
Branches swing with a giggling spree,
Who knew trees could be so carefree?

Squirrels scamper, plotting their play,
On branches where acorns tumble away.
Nature's jesters, they leap and glide,
With laughter hidden in every stride.

The Rapture of Roots and Wings

Roots deep in the soil, they scheme,
To tickle the sky, a soaring dream.
Wings flutter wildly, quite absurd,
Imagining tales that seem unheard.

With whispers of wind that carry a joke,
Even branches join in, a jovial poke.
Nature's chorus, all merry and bright,
Under the sun, they revel in light.

Soliloquy of Treetop Dreams

Up high in the boughs, where giggles abound,
Trees share secrets, their roots underground.
A wise old oak chuckles in thought,
"Why do humans give what they've sought?"

With leaves that rustle like gossiping friends,
Each twig holds a tale that never ends.
In leafy lounges, they ponder away,
While birds chuckle softly, just passing the day.

Blossoms Caught in the Gentle Breeze

Petals like confetti caught in a whirl,
Each bloom in a frolic, a colorful twirl.
They laugh as they fall, a playful descent,
In nature's gala, purely content.

Bees buzz around, joining in the cheer,
As flowers sway low to lend them an ear.
With pollen exchanged, they brew up a tune,
Together they dance under the bright moon.

Nature's Heartstrings in Harmony

In the woods where critters play,
The squirrels dance in bright array.
Each leaf a note upon the breeze,
They twirl with joy among the trees.

A rabbit hops, a raccoon prances,
They all engage in silly glances.
Nature's choir, a merry band,
Conducted by a gentle hand.

The Essence of Earthy Humility

A turtle talks to a wise old toad,
Comparing speeds on a winding road.
"Slow and steady wins!" the toad will yell,
While the turtle smiles, holed in its shell.

Mossy carpets waltz on the ground,
Where mushrooms laugh and twirl around.
With roots that twist and little sprouts,
They giggle softly, there's no doubt!

Choreography of the Windswept Thicket

The willows sway with flirty flair,
Tickled by breezes in the air.
Dancing branches, laughter deep,
While watching saplings start to leap.

A chipmunk joins, it jumps and twirls,
With acorns tossed like tiny pearls.
Nature's ballet, a humorous scene,
Where all the plants are super keen!

Ink of Nature's Palette

The flowers bloom in colors bright,
Each hue a giggle, pure delight.
A bumblebee, with stripes so bold,
Paints the air with tales untold.

With petals soft, they wave and sway,
In the sunshine, come out to play.
Nature's brush, a jester's gift,
With laughter leaves that dance and lift.

The Silhouettes of Dusk's Caress

In shadows deep, the critters dance,
With twinkling stars, they take a chance.
A squirrel slips on acorn's skin,
Cackling loud, it spins to win.

A raccoon juggernauts the grass,
Chasing fireflies as they pass.
But each step is a comic feat,
As muddy paws land on two feet!

The owls hoot, they laugh and jest,
In nightly games, they are the best.
While rabbits plot a grand charade,
To steal carrots with a masquerade.

So gather round, and heed the sound,
Of giggles rich and joy profound.
In dusk's embrace, the fun's begun,
As nature's jesters make their run.

The Golden Touch of Autumn Leaves

Upon the ground, the leaves do swirl,
Like golden coins in a child's world.
A gust of wind brings forth the glee,
As kids jump in to make a spree.

With crunching sounds beneath their feet,
They leap and laugh, a merry beat.
But one slips, tumbles in a heap,
The laughter echoes, oh so steep!

The pumpkins grin, with faces bright,
As squirrels scheme in playful fight.
With hidden nuts and secret plans,
They plot their heist with tiny hands.

So gather 'round the autumn cheer,
Where every leaf brings joy, not fear.
In nature's carnival of hues,
We celebrate the quirky views.

A Blessing from the Enchanted Glade

In a glade where wonders bloom,
The fairies gather, bright with gloom.
They sprinkle laughter, silly charms,
While gnomes devise their crazy farms.

A creature hops with mismatched socks,
While pinching fruit from hidden stocks.
The trees chuckle, their branches sway,
As if to join the games at play.

With whispers soft, they share their tales,
Of cheeky plots and daring sails.
Each leaf carries a giggling breeze,
That tickles all with playful tease.

So wander through this glade of mirth,
Where silliness will find its birth.
A symphony of joy and laughs,
As nature plays with puppet crafts.

Twilight Tales of the Grove

In twilight's glow, the stories weave,
Of critters plotting tricks to leave.
A fox wearing a top hat bold,
Synchronizes moves, oh so cold!

A badger dons a cloak so grand,
With acorn crown upon his hand.
The trees lean in to hear the jest,
As laughter spills, a joyful fest.

With stories shared beneath the moon,
All gather 'round, a happy tune.
As whispers dance on breeze so light,
They toast to friendship, ever bright.

So join the grove, where tales run free,
Of silly pranks and harmony.
In every bark and rustling leaf,
The woodland brings us purest relief.

Harmony Among Ancient Boughs

In a grove where the owls hoot,
The squirrels wear tiny boots.
Branches sway in a silly song,
Leaves giggle, 'Come dance along!'

Nature's jesters, plump and round,
Tumble down, twirling on the ground.
With acorns as their fancy hats,
They prance and play like cheeky brats.

The wise old tree just shakes his bark,
As woodland critters make their mark.
Why so serious, they all tease,
As they frolic in the summer breeze.

So come, let's join the leafy cheer,
With laughter ringing far and near.
In this wood, shenanigans thrive,
Where ancient boughs keep the fun alive!

The Dance of Shadows and Light

Beneath the glow of the moon's soft beam,
The shadows twist, they laugh, they scheme.
Fairy lights flicker, a joyous sight,
As the trees sway, both left and right.

Crickets chirp a raucous beat,
As critters shuffle on tiny feet.
The night invites a grand parade,
In the spotlight where antics are played.

Moonbeams leap like dancers bold,
While branches clap in a dance of old.
Each gust of wind tells a joke,
Happiness swirls in the air, a cloak.

So if you wander 'neath the night sky,
Join the revelry, don't be shy.
For where shadows and laughter reside,
Life's quirks and wonders collide!

Whispers of the Silver Trees

In the huddle of whispers, secrets flow,
The silver trees giggle, just so.
Their branches, all tangled in glee,
Murmur tales of rascally spree.

With every breeze a teasing sound,
They play peek-a-boo with the ground.
"Where did that acorn go?" they jest,
"Under our twigs, take a rest!"

The ladybugs dress like little fools,
With polka dots and wooden stools.
In this lively grove, everyone plays,
Spinning around for endless days.

So wander here, let worries cease,
Among these trees, find perfect peace.
For laughter lingers in daylight's gleam,
And whispers dance like a playful dream!

Underneath the Canopy's Embrace

When the sun peeks through, it's time to play,
While tiny fairies flutter and sway.
The foliage rustles like shuffling feet,
Dreamy dances in nature's heartbeat.

Bumblebees buzz a bumbling tune,
While blossoms sway, swaying in June.
Laughter bubbles through this green chest,
Where tiny creatures know how to jest.

The roots tickle as you stroll by,
Making all the merriment nigh.
Giggles echo under the shade,
In this forest where fun is made.

So roam beneath the leafy sky,
Join the dance of the trees, oh my!
For in this haven of joyous trace,
Life is a dance, a sweet embrace!

An Invocation of Timber's Heart

In the forest, trees like friends,
Whispers dancing as the breeze bends.
A squirrel in a hat, quite the show,
Jumps from branch to branch, oh what a glow!

Roots that tangle, like gossiping mates,
Sharing secrets of nature's fates.
A possum sings in off-key flair,
While the owl just gives a bewildered stare.

Branches sway in a comical waltz,
Nature's clowns, without any faults.
Laughing leaves fall, a fluttering tease,
Joining the chorus of giggling trees.

Here is where mischief dwells at night,
Moonlit shadows dance in pure delight.
A raccoon holds court, with tales so absurd,
Beneath the canopy, the laughter's heard.

The Reverberations of Nature's Breath

Sticks and stones make the wild laugh,
A rabbit critiques, with a sly half.
The turtle winks from his slow parade,
While the wise old woodpecker's charade.

With twigs for pals, the pine trees jest,
Wishing on acorns—they feel so blessed!
Their raucous jokes echo through the glades,
Who knew that timber could throw such shades?

In the pond, the frogs have their say,
Croaking jokes in their own funny way.
While the fish roll their eyes, swim away fast,
As the forest quakes with laughter's blast.

The wind sends tickles to each leafy face,
The harmony of laughter fills every space.
A cheeky breeze whispers "hush!" so sly,
As nature's jesters join in the high-fly.

Enchantment Found in Woodland Shadows

Among the ferns, secrets unfurl,
A shy little gnome, doing a twirl.
His hat is too big, it covers his eyes,
He stumbles and giggles, oh what a surprise!

The shadows weave tales of the day,
Squirrels meeting owls for a nightly soiree.
With nutty punchlines and tales of the trees,
They pull the tricksters with dappled leaves.

A mouse in a vest tips his cheese-topped hat,
While the wise deer chuckles, "Now how about that?"
Fluffy clouds join in, floating with cheer,
Comedic moments, they hold so dear.

Twilight falls, casting giggle and glow,
The forest's alive with a laughable show.
In woodland shadows, joy finds its way,
Through whimsical whispers at the end of the day.

The Ballad of Weathered Trunks

Oh, weathered trunks with stories profound,
Splintered characters gather around.
The benchwarmer logs crinkle with laughs,
Their bark made of giggles, drawn in halves.

Once a grand oak, now slightly bent,
Looking for pinecones to pay his rent.
A jolly old willow with a swaying belt,
Swings his branches, feeling quite felt!

Ferny friends tickle, in patches they hide,
While mossy mischief spreads far and wide.
The troupe of trees, with a skip and a hop,
Chase each other, they never will stop!

Around the rings of ages gone past,
They share crazy tales that forever will last.
In the heart of the grove, where the laughter's thick,
The weathered trunks play their slapstick trick.

A Tapestry of Pale Branches

In a grove where laughter blends,
The branches wiggle like goofy friends.
They whisper secrets, avoid the sun,
Dancing shadows, oh what fun!

A squirrel twirls with acorn flair,
Hitching a ride on the old brown hair.
A twist, a spin, a daring leap,
Nature loves this playful heap.

The breeze joins in, it starts to tease,
Giving each leaf a gentle squeeze.
With every rustle, there's a joke,
Among the trees, bright laughter woke.

So here we sit, in this leafy show,
Where silly winds make mischief flow.
A tapestry spun with chuckles bright,
Beneath the branches, life feels right.

The Forest's Gentle Serenade

In the woods where the laughter reigns,
Whistling winds play playful games.
A rabbit hops with a silly grin,
He twirls and bounces, let the fun begin!

The owls hoot in a mock debate,
"Who's the wisest?" Oh, isn't fate great?
As they blink down with amused surprise,
Nature's comedy, a grand disguise.

The mushrooms giggle in shades of green,
Wobbling lightly, such a silly scene.
Twinkling stars peek through the leaves,
Sharing secrets that the forest weaves.

A playful breeze kicks up some dust,
In this woodland, we can all trust.
To share a laugh, to dance, to sing,
The forest's joy is a wondrous thing.

Fluttering Dreams Beneath the Branches

Beneath the canopy of fluttering dreams,
A butterfly prances, or so it seems.
With wings of joy, it flits so high,
Tickling flowers as it floats by.

Frogs in chorus croak a tune,
Jamming hard by the light of the moon.
With slippery moves, they steal the show,
Jumping and singing, go frogs, go!

Each leaf is bobbing like a silly hat,
While critters giggle, imagine that!
The breeze flows softly, wrapped in cheer,
Stirring up laughter, spreading the cheer.

So come along and sing with grace,
In this whimsical, leafy place.
Fluttering dreams in the air we sway,
Nature's humor lights up the day.

Symphony of the Swaying Boughs

In a symphony, the boughs do sway,
Branches dancing in a merry ballet.
Leaves tapping softly, a rhythmic play,
A delightful tune that brightens the day.

The woodpecker beats on his wooden drum,
A maestro of mischief, oh here he comes!
With every peck, a giggle's found,
In this concert where joy abounds.

The wind's a comedian, twisting about,
Making the flowers wobble and shout.
A honeybee hums, joining the spree,
Buzzing the chorus, happy and free.

So gather 'round for this playful event,
Where nature's marionettes are heaven-sent.
In the sway of the boughs, we find our bliss,
A funny forest, we wouldn't miss.

Beneath the Frosted Veil

Underneath the frosted leaves,
Squirrels dance, oh what a tease!
They scamper here, they frolic there,
Wearing snowflakes like a pair.

The icy grip of winter's chill,
Turned a dance floor, to our thrill.
With every twirl and spin they make,
They laugh and leap, not one mistake.

Chasing shadows, oh so sly,
Why does that pine cone pass them by?
With every skip and silly cheer,
Frosty giggles fill the sphere.

So lift your mugs and toast the trees,
To squirrels, winter, and their tease.
For laughter rings, through frosty air,
Beneath a veil, of frozen care.

In the Company of Timelessness

Time stands still among the oaks,
Whispering secrets, sharing jokes.
The sun peeks through with golden rays,
Lighting up those timeless days.

The shadows stretch, then twist and twine,
Like jesters playing on the line.
With every laugh, the branches sway,
In a comedic, leafy ballet.

Old roots chuckle beneath the ground,
As silly squirrels leap around.
While creatures pause, and birds take flight,
In this grand tale of pure delight.

So dance away, oh merry friends,
In timeless woods where laughter blends.
Underneath the bowing trees,
Life's humorous twist, the gentle breeze.

The Forest's Forgotten Hymn

In shadows deep, the forest sings,
Of forgotten joys and funny flings.
With ancient trees, they sway and sway,
Chasing the clouds, in a whimsy play.

A rabbit prances, quite the sight,
Dressed in leaves, all day and night.
It hops and skips without a care,
While squirrels laugh, tossing in the air.

The brook behind chuckles so clear,
Tickling stones with glee and cheer.
Each ripple echoes in delight,
Transporting joy from day to night.

But listen close to woodpecker's drum,
A rhythm perfect, fun and glum.
In the forest's heart, so rich and grand,
Humor breathes across the land.

Enchanted Silence of the Old Ones

In quiet glens where old ones dwell,
Lies a humor only they can tell.
With knowing grins and twinkling eyes,
They chuckle soft as moonlight sighs.

Their ancient roots intertwined in jest,
Whispering tales of the very best.
The trees don hats, the rocks wear shoes,
In this enchanted place, they can't lose.

The nightingale sings a quirky tune,
While shadows skip beneath the moon.
With every note, the laughter flows,
In secret groves, where mischief grows.

So join the chase, where wisdom meets,
With folly mixed in laughter's beats.
In the silence, humor finds its path,
Among the old ones' merry math.

The Soliloquy of the Green Maid

In a dress of leaves, she twirls with glee,
Singing songs to a bumblebee.
With a wink and a laugh, she spins around,
Chasing shadows on the ground.

Oh, the squirrels giggle and play,
While the chickens join in the fray.
Her laughter rings through the trees,
Like a jester's cheer on the breeze.

She whispers secrets to the sky,
As clouds pass by, much to her sigh.
With flips and hops, she prances bright,
Oh, what a joy to be so light!

Her green crown sways as she leaps,
Gossip of branches, the forest keeps.
In her world of wonder and dream,
Life's silliness flows like a stream.

Beneath the Arched Canopies

Under branches, a jolly scene,
Where every critter's a dancing machine.
Mice find rhythm in the grass,
As insects join their merry class.

Frogs croak tunes with a ribbit so clear,
While fireflies bring the atmosphere.
With a hop and a skip, they dance in a line,
Around the tall trees that twist and entwine.

A raccoon steals the show with flair,
Swapping pies for the fox's stare.
Everyone laughs, it's a cheerful brood,
In the shade of the forest, life is good.

Beneath the arches, chaos reigns,
With joyous antics, life sustains.
Laughter bounces from tree to tree,
In this whimsical world, come dance with me!

Whirlwind Stories of the Bark

Gather 'round for tales of yore,
Where wooden whispers have much in store.
The old oak chuckles, its bark a map,
Of silly storms and a squirrel's mishap.

A rabbit rode a fox one day,
In a race that went astray.
With every hop and every skip,
They found themselves in quite the trip!

The pine trees murmur with each soft gust,
Telling tales of a feathery trust.
Birds on branches laugh and squawk,
As friendships blossom in their talk.

So let the tales swirl like the breeze,
Of forest fun and sugar-sweet leaves.
Every bark holds a giggle or two,
In this whirlwind of stories, fresh as dew.

The Dance of the Swirling Leaves

Round and round, the leaves do swirl,
Spinning tales in a joyful whirl.
With a rustle here and a rustle there,
They chatter to clouds without a care.

A leaf in blue, a leaf in red,
Fell onto a frog, who jumped instead!
With each bounce, a giggle flies,
As colorful crowns fill up the skies.

They hop on breezes like merry sprites,
Mixing with sunbeams and moonlight bites.
A leaf took flight with a twist and a roll,
Declaring, "I'm off for a stroll!"

So join the dance of the swirling show,
Where laughter echoes and spirits glow.
In a world of whimsy, nothing's wrong,
With the leaves' funny dance, come sing along!

Memoirs of a Starlit Grove

In a grove where shadows play,
The trees dance in a quirky sway.
Squirrels chuckle in the night,
As owls hoot with pure delight.

A picnic basket made of leaves,
With acorns piled as if in thieves.
The mushrooms gossip quite a lot,
About the latest forest plot.

In the moonlight, fairies prance,
Teaching frogs how to romance.
A raccoon steals a sweet treat,
While the fireflies tap their feet.

When dawn arrives, the fun won't cease,
For every branch holds tales of peace.
With laughter filling every bough,
The starlit grove takes its bow.

Seasons of the Whispering Woods

In spring, the flowers toss and twirl,
As bees begin their dizzy whirl.
The trees wear crowns of greens so bright,
Swaying gently with pure delight.

Summer brings a T-Rex roar,
As squirrels argue who wants more.
The sunbeams sneak through shady leaves,
While ants host dance-offs, no reprieves.

Autumn dons a jacket of gold,
While the critters share tales old.
With pumpkins rolling all around,
The forest echoes with laughter's sound.

Winter wraps the woods in white,
With snowflakes bursting in sheer flight.
Yet even in the cold of frost,
The spirits party, never lost.

Guardians of the Forest's Heart

In the heart where mysteries dwell,
The guardians laugh, casting a spell.
With twinkling lights that wink and tease,
They shake their leaves like playful trees.

A hedgehog croons a silly tune,
While raccoons swipe snacks under the moon.
The owls hoot their approval loud,
As creatures gather, feeling proud.

Each trunk stands tall, a watcher true,
Of joy and madness, swirling through.
The whispers weave as branches sway,
Inviting all to join the play.

Under stars that shimmer and spark,
The guardians sing till it's dark.
A council of quirky critter fun,
In a forest that never runs.

A Symphony of Branches and Dreams

In the orchestra of rustling leaves,
A symphony of laughter weaves.
The branches strum a merry tune,
While squirrels tap dance under the moon.

A raccoon plays the drums so loud,
As frogs croak proudly, drawing a crowd.
A woodpecker joins in with a beat,
Creating rhythms that can't be beat.

Dreams take flight on the eagle's wings,
While owls advise on silly things.
The flowers sway, tapping their toes,
As everyone joins in, and it shows.

From dawn till dusk, the music flows,
Among the trees where wonder grows.
In this symphony of joy and cheer,
The forest thrives, year after year.

Shadows in the Dappled Light

In the forest bright and green,
Shadows dance, a funny scene.
Wobbling squirrels chase their tails,
Whispering secrets on the trails.

A rooster in a dapper coat,
Tries to sing, but can't quite gloat.
The old owl chuckles, eyes wide,
As he watches the antics glide.

Frogs leap high with joyful glee,
While rabbits hop as wild as can be.
Underneath the leafy shade,
The laughter of the trees won't fade.

Each rustle brings another jest,
Nature plays, she knows her best.
With giggles from the branches near,
The forest echoes, "Come hang here!"

When the Wind Calls the Wood

When the wind begins to play,
Leaves reply, come join the fray.
A cheeky breeze makes branches sway,
Sending acorns down the way.

The chipmunks skitter all about,
Chasing wind, they scream and shout.
One trips over a fallen twig,
With a flop, he does a jig.

The pine trees start to giggle loud,
Rustling clothing, swaying proud.
A squirrel snatches a gusty treat,
And tumbles down, then jumps to his feet.

All around, the mischief calls,
Nature's laughter fills the halls.
When the wind blows, join the crew,
In the woods, there's fun for you!

Nature's Tender Elegy

In the forest filled with cheer,
Nature sings, we want to hear.
A thistle tickles a passing deer,
As she prances without fear.

The sun peeks through the trees' embrace,
As mushrooms pop up in a race.
A frog in a crown leaps with flair,
Declaring himself the king of air.

Bees are buzzing all around,
In search of sweets that can be found.
One bumbles and lands on a nose,
The giggles fly where humor grows.

Underneath the bright sky's dome,
Every creature feels at home.
A gentle tease, a playful jest,
Nature's joy is simply the best!

Veils of Mist Amongst the Thickets

Veils of mist, a curious sight,
Goblins peek, then dash in fright.
A laughing breeze twirls the fog,
Spying on a sleepy dog.

The thickets rustle, secrets shared,
A rabbit whispers, all prepared.
With a wink and a jolly hop,
He challenges the clouds to stop!

The echoes of a distant shout,
Brought the critters all about.
The fox with shades and a sly grin,
Announced the party, let's begin!

With misty veils, the stories spin,
Where laughter lives, and fun begins.
In every nook, a giggle hides,
Amongst the thickets, joy resides.

An Ode to the Silver Trunks

Silver trunks in the sun, just peeking,
They sway with joy, like they're speaking.
Leaves like laughter rustling so loud,
Dancing dumbly, oh so proud.

Squirrels prance with acorn hats,
Trying to dodge the playful bats.
Birds chirp jokes from branches high,
While the wind just whooshes by.

One trunk tripped, oh what a sight,
Fell for a root in pure delight.
Laughter echoed through the grove,
As tree-friends gathered, jokes they wove.

A picnic planned by roots and vines,
With fuzzy nuts and wild grape wines.
By sunset's brush, they show their glee,
In nature's jest, they all agree.

In the Stillness of Timbered Souls

In hushed woods where shadows creep,
The trees make grins, though roots are deep.
With woeful leaves, they tell a tale,
Of gales and gusts that made them pale.

A squirrel joked, 'I'm quite the spry,'
When winds blew hard, oh my, oh my!
His acorn hat flew past the pines,
And laughter brewed in tangled lines.

Old oaks grumble, 'What's that fuzz?'
Referring to the bushes' buzz.
Their bark breaks smiles across the way,
'The sun's our friend,' they seem to say.

Through silent laughter, branches sway,
Winking at clouds, they play all day.
In quiet woods where spirits dance,
Laughter echoes, their hearts' romance.

Celestial Harmonies Between the Trees

Underneath the skies so bright,
Trees join in a laughter fight.
Branches strum with wind as notes,
While nature's chorus gaily floats.

A raccoon sings a silly tune,
To the rhythm of the glowing moon.
Boughs sway gently, join the fun,
As stars blink bright, one by one.

The forest floor, a stage well set,
For shadow plays and a sunset bet.
With twirling leaves and swooping bats,
They dance along with goofy hats.

Even the old pine winks his eye,
As the nightingale sings low and sly.
In harmony, they share their cheer,
Nature's laughter, ever near.

Song of the Moonlit Glade

In the moonlit glade where giggles grow,
Trees shake hands with breezes that blow.
Whispers of secrets swirl with the night,
And critters engage in a playful fight.

A wise old tree, with knobby knees,
Tells jokes that rustle the leafy breeze.
Mossy cushions for all to ponder,
While stars above spread joy and wonder.

Fireflies flash like wild applause,
As owls swoon with a leisurely yawn.
Branches weave tales of laughter's tune,
Joined by the mischief of the raccoon.

With echoes of cheer, the night winds roll,
As nature hums a balmy soul.
In the moonlit glade, a joy parade,
Where every laugh's a serenade.

The Dance of Frost and Flame

In the chill of the night, frosty feet,
A fireball twirls, oh what a feat!
Flames doing the tango, sparks fly bright,
Frost giggles in shadows, slipping from sight.

Sassy little embers jump with glee,
Challenging frost in their merry spree.
A snowflake waltzes; 'Come dance with me!'
Yet each takes a tumble, oh how funny to see!

A frost and a flame, they chase in a loop,
Creating a scene, a whimsical troupe.
One slips on a patch of icy delight,
While the other roasts marshmallows, what a sight!

And as dawn breaks with a bright, silly grin,
Frost bows to the flame, "Oh, let me in!"
They laugh at the morning, their dance done in jest,
A quirky duet that simply feels blessed.

Serenity Beneath the Verdant Dome

Under the branches where squirrels convene,
A leaf fell down, looking quite serene.
It whispered to flowers, 'Join in my game!'
But petals just giggled, 'We're not new to fame!'

The sun peeked in, with a wink and bright cheer,
The grass tickled toes, 'Stay longer, my dear!'
With a rustle of leaves, laughter took flight,
As shadows played hopscotch, what a sight!

A rabbit broke in, thinking it's grand,
To join the parade of this leafy band.
Yet tripped on a root, oh what a blunder,
He tumbled and rolled, beneath all the thunder!

In this emerald world, life dances and plays,
With every small mishap, joyfully stays.
Beneath the green dome, the fun never ends,
Nature's own comedy, full of silly bends!

Fragments of a Sunlit Path

On a sunlit path where shadows loom,
A butterfly giggles and dances in bloom.
It trips on a twig, then gives a loud squeal,
Pondering life—'Is this how I feel?'

A hedgehog nearby, rolling in style,
Stops to observe, with a curious smile.
"Oh dear, dear butterfly, why such a rush?"
She laughed, 'Just trying to avoid the big mush!'

The sun beams down with a playful warm grin,
As petals join in, and the laughter begins.
'Let's skip down the trail!' calls a cheeky old crow,
But trips on a branch—a comedy show!

Each creature now dancing in joyous delight,
Nature's own folly, oh what a sight!
With each little stumble and giggle they find,
Life's a fun journey, so jest and unwind!

The Resilience of the Wooded Heart

In a forest of laughter, tall trees joke loud,
With branches like arms, thrilled to be proud.
A squirrel drops acorns, rolling with glee,
Making hats for the rabbits; 'Come play with me!'

The wise old owl hoots with a tone quite absurd,
'What's going on here? Have you all heard?
This isn't a party—it's just bedtime now!'
But a fox piped up, 'Oh, just take a bow!'

Under the canopy, mischief takes flight,
As twinkling stars peek in to delight.
A moonbeam whispers, 'Come join our ball!'
Leaves swirl in waltzes, responding to the call!

With each little jest that the woodland sees,
Life thrives with laughter on every breeze.
In resilience they play, hearts merry and bright,
In a world full of whimsy, they twirl through the night!

Rhythms of the Dancing Saplings

In the meadow, small trees sway,
With whispers of joy, they play.
A squirrel tries to join the fun,
But trips on roots, oh what a run!

Little leaves spin in delight,
As branches twirl through the night.
The owls hoot, a curious crowd,
For who knew saplings danced so loud?

Their laughter carried on the breeze,
While rabbits giggle near the trees.
Nature's jesters, swift and spry,
Who knew they'd leap and touch the sky!

With every jig, a critter grins,
The forest bops, and chaos begins.
They dance on roots, as shadows flick,
Behold the woods, where laughter's thick!

The Guardians of the Glade

In the glade, the critters scheme,
Watchful eyes like a dream team.
A raccoon wearing a tiny hat,
Claims he's the king, imagine that!

Squirrels chatter, a raucous sound,
As they gather round and around.
They plot and plan with much delight,
Guardians of fun till the night!

The hedgehogs roll in ball-like form,
Creating mischief, oh so warm.
With thorns like armor, they rush around,
A prickly charge, ready to astound!

The owls laugh from their leafy thrones,
At the chaos stirred by furry clones.
Together they guard, with goofy pride,
In this glade where laughter can't hide!

Timeless Secrets of the Forest

In the woods, secrets abound,
Only the trees have truly found.
A wise old oak, with gnarled bark,
Shares jokes that light up the dark!

The ferns giggle, a hidden crew,
Whispering tales, both old and new.
A pine cone rolls with a silly pace,
And bumps a rabbit right in the face!

Crickets chirp a merry tune,
While flowers sway beneath the moon.
Nature's humor, bright and free,
In every nook, a chuckle's key!

In these woods, the laughter flows,
As each creature with mischief glows.
Together they share the timeless jest,
In the forest's heart, we find our best!

Flickering Lanterns of the Wild

In the wild, where shadows dance,
Fireflies twinkle, a lighted prance.
Amidst the ferns, they dart and dive,
With each flicker, the night comes alive!

A raccoon tries to catch a glow,
But oh! That sneaky firefly's a pro.
With a giggle, it zips away,
Turning the chase into a play!

The raccoon's charm, a sight to see,
With mud on paws, so carefree.
Beneath the moon, mischief brews,
As each little lantern hums the blues!

The night becomes a carnival scene,
With every light, a cheeky sheen.
In the wild, laughter ignites,
With flickering lanterns, dancing lights!

Echoing Through the Quiet Woods

In the woods, where echoes play,
The trees dance like they're in a ballet.
Squirrels giggle in the leafy shade,
As branches whisper jokes they've made.

A deer trots past, a comedian bold,
With antlers wearing a crown of gold.
Leaves rustle like a clapping crowd,
As laughter floats, oh so loud!

A fox roams in with a sneaky grin,
Telling tales of his latest win.
The owls hoot 'til they're dizzy and spun,
While the wind joins in, just having fun.

So if you wander through this glade,
Listen close, don't let it fade.
For in the woods, the jokes don't stop,
Just when you think it's time to hop.

Memory of the Swaying Delicacy

Once danced a tree with limbs so light,
In the breeze, oh what a sight!
She swayed and twirled as if on stage,
Her leaves throwing a leafy rage.

A chipmunk laughed at her wobbly feat,
'This tree thinks she's a dainty treat!'
The sunlight twinkled, teasing her sway,
As if to say, 'Don't go away!'

Even the mushrooms began to clap,
To the rhythm of her leafy rap.
And all the critters in a row,
Joined in the fun, putting on a show!

So remember when you pass this way,
The dancing tree's funny display.
For in nature's arms, joy is grand,
A swaying delicacy, so unplanned.

In the Heart of the Whispering Grove

In the grove, where whispers roam,
Trees gossip like they're at home.
A squirrel said, 'Did you see him swerve?'
'The way he tripped, oh how we served!'

With a rustle, the branches chimed,
'Oh dear, that fella's truly blind!'
While the ferns giggled, they swayed to and fro,
As the sun peeked down with a playful glow.

A rabbit hopped in, taking the stage,
His jokes, you'd think, came from a page.
'Life's a hop, then a tumble,' he said,
'Just look at the trees—green overhead!'

So come and listen, let it be known,
In this grove, the laughter has grown.
For in every rustle and fluttering leaf,
Lies a joke that brings sweet relief.

The Pantomime of the Wandering Branches

A branch began to strut and sway,
Putting on a show, come what may.
With every twist, the critters cheered,
'Our leafy hero, how he steered!'

The bark stood tall, with humor deep,
'Join my act, it's fun, no sleep!'
Then twirled the vines, a tangled mess,
'This is relaxation, I confess!'

A butterfly flitted, joining the plot,
'Don't leave me out; I can dance a lot!'
The sun beamed down, laughing with glee,
As shadows danced in harmony.

So in this theater of green delight,
The branches perform from day to night.
If you wander here, be sure to glance,
At the trees that laugh and prance.

The Portrait of Seasons in Leaves

In springtime's dance, the leaves are fresh,
They twirl and swirl, in colors meshed.
A gust of wind, they take to flight,
Chasing each other, what a sight!

Summer sun's here, they bask and play,
With laughing branches, they sway all day.
A picnic beneath, crumbs all around,
A feast for the squirrels, oh, what a sound!

Autumn arrives, they wear banners bright,
Orange and red, such a silly sight.
They drop like confetti, a colorful rain,
Joyful and jolly, no sign of pain!

Winter shows up, with a chilly grin,
Covered in snow, they chuckle within.
Staying cozy, dancing in frost,
Sipping hot chocolate, they're never lost!

Tales Woven in the Rustic Fiber

Rustic fibers twist and twine,
Whispering secrets in the sunshine.
Gossiping leaves with a wink and twist,
Plotting adventures in a sunrise mist.

A squirrel's tale of grandeur spun,
Acorns hidden, all in fun.
Leaves play dress-up, a carnival show,
Neighbors laugh at the leaves' little blow.

A mouse strolls by with a puzzled glance,
At the leaves' bizarre little dance.
What's up with the grass, a ticklish joke,
When the daffodils giggle and poke?

Even the branches join in the glee,
A tree stand-up, oh what a spree!
In the rustic weave, all stories align,
Nature's comedy, oh so fine!

After the Storm: A Tree's Reflection

The storm passed by, a wild affair,
With branches flailing like wild hair.
Raindrops danced like tiny clowns,
Tickling the leaves, they spun around.

Peeking out, the sun has won,
Rainbow smiles, it's all in fun!
Trees lean in to share a laugh,
While puddles sway, a wobbly raft.

Birds tweet tales of weathered strife,
In watery mirrors, they find new life.
The bark's been scrubbed, a shiny show,
A tree makeover, don't you know?

Roots chuckle softly beneath the ground,
In nature's whimsy, joy is found.
After the storm, with laughter bright,
A tree reflects, all feels just right!

Garden of Poised Silence

In a garden where silence plays,
Flowers giggle in sun-kissed rays.
With whispers soft, the petals sing,
In a waltz of quiet, they truly spring.

The daisies gossip, oh what a crew,
While ferns feign grace, trying too.
The roses blush, in vibrant hue,
Making faces, it's all brand new!

Worms slither by with a snicker or two,
While crickets join in, with a hoppy woo.
Every leaf a storyteller bold,
In this garden, laughter unfolds.

Underneath the moon, quiet and sweet,
The blooms make jokes, never miss a beat.
In this poised silence, joy is the aim,
Nature's comedy, never the same!

Whispers of the Silver Leaves

In the forest, leaves do chat,
One says, "Look, a silly cat!"
Swaying softly, bending low,
They laugh at how the breezes blow.

A squirrel darts, in search of food,
While mushrooms dance, in a merry mood.
The branches wiggle, tickled by air,
As trees tell jokes, without a care.

A woodpecker knocks with such great flair,
Who knew that laughter filled the air?
With every tap, a giggle flows,
In nature's play, everybody knows.

So gather 'round, each critter, mate,
In the tree's embrace, celebrate!
For life is fun beneath the sun,
Where silver leaves say, "Join the fun!"

Beneath the Canopy's Embrace

Beneath the boughs, a gathering spins,
With acorns rolling, laughter begins.
The branches tap out a merry beat,
As chipmunks shuffle their tiny feet.

A frog croaks loud, "I can dance, too!"
While crickets chirp, "Well, I can woo!"
The sun peeks down, with a teasing grin,
Nature's party is set to begin!

A raccoon grins, wearing his mask,
"Who's the best dancer?" is the nightly task.
The moon beams down, a spotlight bright,
While leaves all rustle with pure delight.

So join the fun, let worries cease,
In the canopy's giggles, find your peace.
For every whisper among the trees,
Is a call to dance, a chance to please!

Lament of the Shivering Bark

Oh bark so old, your stories crack,
Of squirrels chasing, and a wild raccoon pack.
You shudder in laughter, shake with glee,
As the wind jokes past, like a dancing bee.

But lo! Here comes the rain to play,
The puddles splash in a frolicking way.
"Oh dear!" sighs bark, as water does slip,
"Where's my umbrella? Oh, what a trip!"

The splashes giggle as they leap,
While trees, in tune, do sway and creep.
Each drop a chuckle, a playful spark,
Transforming sadness to a jolly lark.

So raise a smile from deep within,
For every shiver hides a grin.
In nature's arms where laughter flows,
Even the oldest bark knows how to glow!

Echoes of the Woodland Anthem

The woods resound with a joyful shout,
As critters gather, there's no doubt.
Beetles march to a beat so fine,
While fireflies twinkle, stars align.

A rabbit hops with style and flair,
"Just try to catch me if you dare!"
The sun drops low, the shadows play,
And laughter rings in a dreamy sway.

The owls chuckle, wise and old,
Their tales of mischief, all retold.
"Who hooted louder?" they like to tease,
As the night whispers through the trees.

So join the choir of woodland cheer,
With every laugh, the world feels near.
In echoes of joy, forever stay,
For the forest sings a silly ballet!

A Chronicle in Each Ring and Leaf

In forest laughter, trees do sway,
Their rings tell tales in a funny way.
Leaves rustle secrets, giggles hide,
As squirrels conduct a woodsy ride.

Raindrops dance in a splendid spin,
Up they go, let the fun begin!
A twig's a wand, a leaf's a hat,
Nature's jesters, imagine that!

Beneath the bark, a joke or two,
Whispers of woodpeckers break through.
Each knot and gnarled twist, a jest,
In every branch, the trees are blessed.

So listen close as you stroll or roam,
In this leafy stage, you'll feel at home.
With every rusted leaf's delight,
The woodlands laugh through day and night.

Ephemeral Echoes of Skylit Woods

The leaves, they chuckle, crisp and bright,
As shadows play in the fading light.
A breeze with humor tickles the trees,
Whispering jokes on the gentle breeze.

Up high, the squirrels motion and prance,
In their nutty world, they take a chance.
With acorns rolling, they joke and chatter,
In their woodland circus, nothing's the matter.

Glimmers of sunlight, dancing about,
Bring out the giggles, the joyful shout.
Mushrooms huddle with mirthful pride,
In this woodland stage, nothing's denied.

So swing on branches, let laughter soar,
In this skylit wonder, who could ask for more?
Each echo rings with a cheerful song,
In the woods where the funny belong.

Remnants of Twilight's Glow

In twilight's glow, the funny tales,
Of chirping crickets and fluttering gales.
Old logs giggle, while shadows do stretch,
As night weaves humor that nature etched.

Frogs croak rhymes in the moon's sweet light,
Jumping about in a comic flight.
Butterflies twirl in their silly dance,
Under the stars, they take the chance.

The owl hoots a punchline, wise and clear,
As raccoons plot their midnight cheer.
In rustling leaves, the laughter grows,
For every creature knows how it goes.

So wander softly, let your heart know,
The remnants of joy, in twilight's glow.
Every whisper, every hoot,
Brings forth the smiles, oh what a hoot!

Secrets Hidden in Wood and Leaf

In shadows deep, secrets hide away,
The trees conspire, having their play.
With roots entwined, they plot and scheme,
Creating humor, a woodland dream.

A fox grins slyly, with mischief abound,
While rabbits giggle, hopping around.
Each rustle of leaves, a playful jest,
In this leafy realm, they dance with zest.

The pinecones tease with a prickly laugh,
As chipmunks scurry on a funny path.
The secrets unfold like nature's grin,
With every bark, the fun begins.

So pause awhile, beneath the green,
In wood and leaf, joy can be seen.
The whispers, the chuckles, the tales they weave,
In nature's heart, there's always reprieve.

Shadows Cradled by the Canopy

In the shade of leafy dreams,
The squirrels dance in silly schemes.
With acorns falling, so many a pound,
They gather nuts all around!

Mice in hats, a bustling crew,
Planting seeds for a veggie stew.
But instead of peas, they find a shoe,
And debate on what they should do.

A fox winks, and joins the plot,
Offers berries from a very odd spot.
They feast and giggle, forget their strife,
A woodland party, oh what a life!

And as the sun doth start to fade,
They dance on roots that nature made.
With every twist and jolly shout,
They keep the forest laughing out!

The Elegy of the Woodland Spirits

Whispers swirl in breezy gusts,
As tiny spirits share their trusts.
With giggles hidden 'neath the leaves,
They play tricks that no one believes!

A gnome with shoes a size too small,
Tripped over mushrooms — who could recall?
He rolled and tumbled, what a sight,
The fairies chuckled with pure delight!

A crow with a very crooked beak,
Tells tall tales that make spirits peek.
They gather close, silvery glow,
And laugh at the stories he bestow!

But when the moonrise starts to swell,
They trap their laughter in a spell.
In shadows deep, their joy takes flight,
Leaving echoes of giggles in the night!

Tales Told by the Rustling Foliage

Underneath the swaying trees,
The breeze tells tales with such ease.
A critter's prank, a shadow's jest,
Nature's laughter, truly blessed!

A beetle dressed in grand attire,
Thought he could fly — but fell, oh dire!
With every thud, the laughter grew,
The flowers giggled, they knew the cue.

Saplings whisper secrets bright,
Of funny happenings in the night.
A raccoon dons a bandit mask,
In search for snacks, it's quite the task!

With chatter soft and rustling sound,
All creatures gather, joy abound.
Together they weave the tales of fun,
In the forest, laughter's never done!

Reverie in the Glade

In a glade where laughter swells,
A rabbit sings of mischief spells.
Pranced and jived in sunny light,
A merry band, oh what a sight!

The hedgehog rolled, then got stuck tight,
A pinecone foe, with all its might.
His friends they gathered, one by one,
And burst with giggles, oh what fun!

The turtle shared a daring joke,
About a silly frog who spoke.
His hopping tales of lofty dreams,
Sent every creature to the streams!

As stars peek through the leafy seams,
They dance and twirl, fulfilling dreams.
In nature's heart, their spirits soar,
In reverie, they laugh some more!

The Echoing Heartbeat of Nature

In the woods, a squirrel pranced bold,
Chasing dreams of acorns untold.
His dance was a jig, a whimsical sight,
Leaves twirled around him, oh, what a flight!

Beneath the front porch, a raccoon swayed,
Dressed in a mask, in mischief he played.
With a twist and a turn, he'd steal a snack,
A cookie or two, then off with a crack!

The rabbit guffaws, with each little hop,
Telling the tales as he reaches the top.
"Carrots are gold, if you know where to dig,
But never forget, a fox likes a jig!"

And so in the woods, with grand symphony,
Nature's heartbeat echoes, noisy and free.
With laughter and jest, the critters conspire,
In a whimsical dance, they never tire.

A Canopy of Secrets Unraveled

In the rustling leaves, the gossip flows,
A secret revealed, the canopy knows.
The owls are chuckling, all wise in their ways,
While the raccoons conspire with scheming displays.

A chittering chorus, the birds start to sing,
Of nuts and of seeds, and the joy they bring.
Rabbits hop past, with noses in air,
"Who needs a garden when life is so fair?"

A sneaky old fox, with a wink and a grin,
Prowls through the thicket, prepared for his win.
"Who's quicker, my dear, is it you or the breeze?"
The trees shake their branches, sharing the tease.

Under the moonlight, while shadows do creep,
The woodland creatures have secrets to keep.
With laughter and joy, they dance in delight,
In this canopy laughter, the world feels just right.

The Soliloquy of a Silent Grove

In the silent grove, a tree spoke aloud,
"Mice dream of cheese, oh, how they're so proud.
But take a good look, my friends, can you see?
My branches extend, as wise as can be!"

A crow cawed out, in his feathery suit,
"Your wisdom is silly, oh, what a hoot!
I'll rule the sky, while you stand so still,
But trees make the best chairs, if you've got the will!"

The grass swayed and giggled, a ticklish affair,
As a worm wiggled up, without any care.
"I'm the sage of the soil, don't mind me, I dwell,
With stories of roots, oh, I know them so well!"

The branches all nodded, leaves fluttered with cheer,
In the silent grove, together they steer.
With laughter and quirks, they fill the cool night,
In the sage's soliloquy, our hearts feel so light.

Whispers of Age in the Woods

In the depths of the woods, the old trees convene,
Sharing tales of the past, a colorful scene.
The whispers of age mingle laughs with the sighs,
While ants march along, in neat little lines.

A beaver chuckles, with logs piled high,
"Building a dam? I'll give it a try!
With splashes and plops, I'll dance down the stream,
Creating a splash, oh, it's all quite a dream!"

The wise old owl hoots, with a mischievous glance,
"Watch out for that squirrel, he's lost in his dance!
With acorns a-flying, he's lost all his grace,
But we love all his antics, his curious pace."

Thus the woods echo secrets, both funny and old,
In the whispers of age, their stories unfold.
With chuckles and giggles, the summers roll by,
In this playful embrace, how time seems to fly!

www.ingramcontent.com/pod-product-compliance
Lightning Source LLC
Chambersburg PA
CBHW071845160426
43209CB00003B/422